WATERLOO LOCAL
MIDDLE SCHOOL LIBRARY

soccer

Consultant

Gene Kenney, soccer coach
Michigan State University
East Lansing, Michigan

Demonstrators

George K. Janes
Rudy Mayer

published by:
The Athletic Institute
Merchandise Mart, Chicago

A not-for-profit organization devoted to the advancement of athletics, physical education and recreation.

Robert G. Bluth, *editor*

© The Athletic Institute 1971
All Rights Reserved

Library of Congress
Catalog Card Number 79-109498

"Sports Techniques" Series
SBN 87670-043-1

Published by The Athletic Institute
Chicago, Illinois 60654

Foreword

The SPORTS TECHNIQUES SERIES is but one item in a comprehensive list of sports instructional aids which are made available by The Athletic Institute. This book is part of a master plan which seeks to make the benefits of athletics, physical education and recreation available to everyone.

The Athletic Institute is a not-for-profit organization devoted to the advancement of athletics, physical education and recreation. The Institute believes that participation in athletics and recreation has benefits of inestimable value to the individual and to the community.

The nature and scope of the many Institute programs are determined by a *Professional Advisory Committee,* whose members are noted for their outstanding knowledge, experience and ability in the fields of athletics, physical education and recreation.

The Institute believes that through this book the reader will become a better performer, skilled in the fundamentals of this fine game. Knowledge and the practice necessary to mold knowledge into playing ability are the keys to real enjoyment in playing any game or sport.

The game of soccer aids in the development of motor skill, flexibility, agility and endurance as well as providing enjoyable recreation.

Donald E. Bushore
Executive Director
The Athletic Institute

Introduction

Soccer is the world's most popular sport for both participation and viewing. The sport links virtually every country on earth with a common language and interest. It is truly the *international sport*.

In nearly every country of the world, the sport is called *football* but in the United States it is known as *soccer*. Soccer combines the continuous action and some of the strategy of hockey, the teamwork of basketball, the timing of baseball, some of the body contact of football and the stamina required for long-distance running. It is a sport whose participants need not be exceptionally tall, such as basketball; or exceptionally big, such as football. Soccer is a sport in which the smaller man can excel, and usually does, with the average player's height ranging between 5'8" and 5'10" and weight being between 145 and 160 pounds.

Interest in soccer in this country has increased tremendously within the past 15 years with the fastest growth seen in the schools and colleges. Many schools cannot finance the fall sport of football. Such schools field varsity soccer teams which have much lower operational costs. Another plus factor is that even with frequent body contact and the small amount of padding used, injuries are surprisingly few.

Children of all ages enjoy playing the game because kicking is a natural activity for youngsters. Soccer is a team game where everybody handles the ball many times during a contest, therefore all must know how to kick, trap, pass, shoot, clear and head. Only the goalkeeper is eligible to catch a ball with his hands and this is allowed only in the penalty area.

Needless to say, the growth in popularity of soccer in our schools, colleges and recreation programs all over the country has enabled the sport to take its place with the other sports which have contributed to our American way of life.

Rules and regulations for schools and colleges can be obtained by purchasing an NCAA guide. These rules differ only slightly from international rules which can be obtained from the United States Soccer Football Association. (See Rules Simplified, page 51).

Gene Kenney

Table of Contents

the kick
Kicking with Inside of Foot Techniques 7
Inside of Instep Techniques 8
Full Instep Kick Techniques 10
Outside of Instep Techniques 11
Volley Kick Techniques 12
Half-Volley Kick Techniques 13
Back Heeling Techniques 14
trapping ground balls
Sole of Foot Techniques 16
Inside of Foot Techniques 17
Outside of Instep Techniques 18
trapping balls in mid-air
Inside of Foot Techniques 20
Instep Techniques 20
Thigh Techniques 22
Chest Trap Techniques 23
heading and backheading
Heading Techniques 25
Backheading Techniques 27
dribbling
Dribbling Techniques 29
Single Feint Techniques 30
Double Feint Techniques 31
tackling
Tackling Techniques 33
Shoulder Tackle Techniques 34
Sliding Tackle Techniques 35
the throw-in
Throw-in Techniques 37
goalkeeper catching
Catching Ground Ball Head On 39
Catching Ground Balls to the Side 40
Catching Medium-High Balls 41
Catching Overhead Balls 42
Punching Ball and Deflecting Ball Over Crossbar Techniques 43
Diving for High Balls and Low Balls 44
goalkeeper clearing
Underhand Clearing Techniques 47
Overhead Clearing Techniques 48
Punt Clearing Techniques 49
rules simplified
Diagram of Field 50
Sources of Soccer Rules 51
Basic Rules of Soccer 51
basic tactics 54
systems of play 58
External Factors Which Affect the Game 62
Helpful Hints for Players 63
glossary of soccer terms 65

the kick

To kick the ball along the ground, extend the force of the kick through the midline of the ball. If struck below the midline, the ball will loft. Generally, if the knee is over the ball at the point of contact, the ball stays low, along the ground. To loft the ball start the kick a little in back of the ball and contact the ball on the upswing. Practice kicks with a stationary ball first, then practice with a moving ball. Always keep your eyes on the ball.

Kicking with Inside of Foot Techniques

With eyes on ball, stride forward placing left foot alongside and six inches away from ball. At this point the left knee is bent slightly to allow weight to go forward on this foot. The right foot or kicking foot is turned outward. Notice as the right foot swings slightly backward it is lifted from ground. Swing the right foot forward forcefully using a push type action. Do not jab. Strike the ball at the midpoint for a low pass or kick. At this point the body will be leaning slightly backward at the hip. Continue a good follow-through with the kicking leg.

1. KEEP EYES ON BALL.

2. PLANT NON-KICKING FOOT ALONGSIDE BALL.

3. WEIGHT ON NON-KICKING FOOT. TURN KICKING FOOT OUTWARD.

4. CONTACT BALL WITH INSIDE OF FOOT.

5. FOLLOW THROUGH.

Inside of Instep Techniques

Inside of instep kicking is one of the most widely used kicks. This kick can be used for cross-field passes, centers, clearances, shots and swerved passes.

When kicking with the right foot, approach the ball from the left at an angle not more than 45 degrees from the direction which the ball will take. Place the non-kicking foot about even with the ball and nine to ten inches away. To loft the ball, place the non-kicking foot slightly behind the ball.

With the left leg bent slightly at the knee and the body leaning away from the kicking foot, bend the upper portion of the body slightly forward. The upper body and the arms will help maintain balance. As you swing the kicking leg backward at the knee, turn the leg outward.

Bring the kicking leg forward with the knee slightly bent and the toe pointing outward and downward. On the follow-through straighten the knee and swing the leg through, extending the kick from the hip.

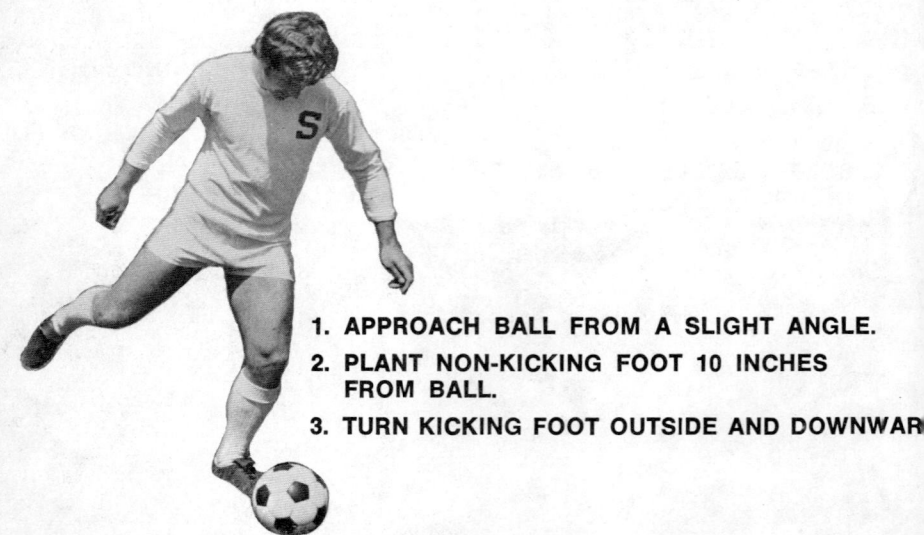

1. APPROACH BALL FROM A SLIGHT ANGLE.
2. PLANT NON-KICKING FOOT 10 INCHES FROM BALL.
3. TURN KICKING FOOT OUTSIDE AND DOWNWAR

The Height of the Kick Depends on Two Factors:

1. Where the Instep Contacts the Ball.

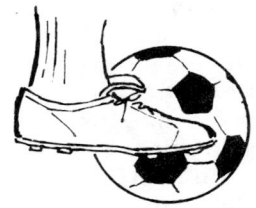 

(CENTER OF BALL FOR LOW KICKS — BELOW CENTER FOR LOBS)

2. The Degree of Backward Inclination.

4. KEEP EYES ON BALL.
5. LEAN BODY AWAY FROM KICKING FOOT.
6. BEND UPPER BODY SLIGHTLY FORWARD.
7. CONTACT BALL INSIDE OF INSTEP.
8. FOLLOW THROUGH.

Full Instep Kick Techniques

This kick is used for passing, clearing and shooting at the goal.

Step directly at ball, placing non-kicking foot alongside and six to eight inches away from the ball. Make sure the toe of the kicking foot is turned down for a low drive and the knee is over the ball at contact. Make contact on top of instep directly over the shoelaces. For a medium or high ball, the knee should be behind the ball upon contact. Use the full instep kick while the ball is still in the air. On this volley shot make sure you are well over the ball and not leaning back.

 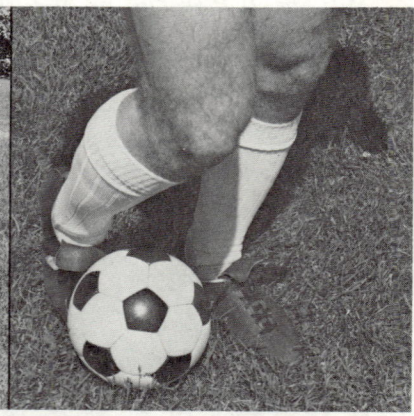

1. KEEP EYES ON BALL.
2. PLANT NON-KICKING FOOT 6-8 INCHES FROM BALL.
3. TURN KICKING TOE DOWNWARD.
4. CONTACT BALL ON TOP OF INSTEP.

Outside of Instep Techniques

Kicking with the *outside of the instep* is very popular because this part of the foot provides a flat kicking surface. This kick allows a variety of shots and passes. The ball can be made to swerve goalward on corner kicks or away from the goalkeeper on any angle shots.

When approaching the ball in a direct line, place the non-kicking foot alongside and six to eight inches away from ball. Turn the kicking foot inward and downward at contact.

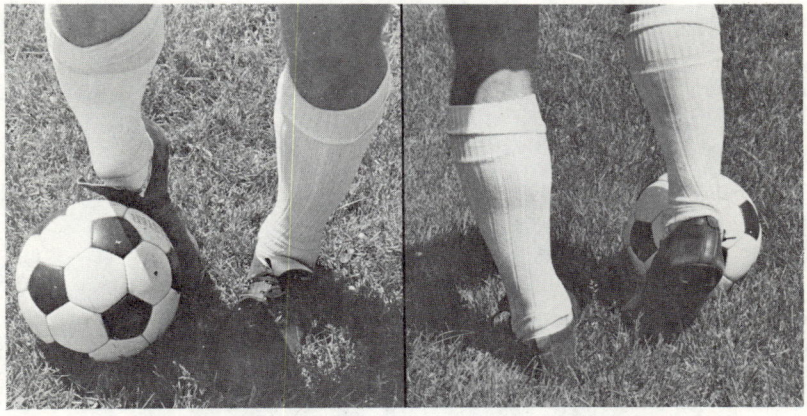

1. PLANT NON-KICKING FOOT 6-8 INCHES FROM BALL.
2. TURN KICKING FOOT DOWNWARD AND INWARD.
3. CONTACT BALL ON OUTSIDE OF INSTEP.
4. FOLLOW THROUGH.

Volley Kick Techniques

The *volley kick* is used for low drives, lofts and for clearances when there isn't time to trap the ball. The ball is kicked while in the air before it touches the ground.

When a low drive is desired, contact the ball close to the ground. Keep your knee and body weight over the ball. Contact the ball on the backside.

1. KEEP EYES ON BALL.
2. POSITION KNEE AND BODY WEIGHT OVER BALL FOR LOW KICK.
3. TO LOFT BALL, LEAN BACK AND CONTACT BALL ON UNDERSIDE.

Half-Volley Kick Techniques

Contact the ball just after it hits the ground to kick the ball on the *half volley*. Apply same techniques as for the volley kick.

1. KEEP EYES ON BALL.
2. FOR LOW KICK, CONTACT BALL ON BACKSIDE CLOSE TO GROUND. KEEP KNEE AND WEIGHT OVER BALL.
3. TO LOFT THE BALL, LEAN BACK AND CONTACT BALL ON UNDERSIDE.

Back Heeling Techniques

Used for short distance passes when running in a direction opposite to the intended pass.

Place non-kicking foot alongside the ball. Pass the kicking foot over the ball. As the foot is brought backward, flex the knee. Contact the ball with the heel.

1. PLACE NON-KICKING FOOT ALONGSIDE BALL.
2. PASS KICKING FOOT OVER BALL.
3. BRING KICKING FOOT BACK WITH KNEE FLEXED.
4. CONTACT BALL WITH HEEL.

trapping ground balls

Trapping means stopping a ground ball or a ball in the air and bringing the ball under control. For most situations, this is accomplished best by slightly recoiling that part of the body trapping the ball.

Sole of Foot Techniques

Face the oncoming ball with your eyes on the ball. Hold the sole of trapping foot obliquely and wedge the ball between ground and sole. Keep the heel close to ground as the ball makes contact. The trapping foot should recoil slightly.

1. KEEP EYES ON BALL.

2. BEND KNEE — DEPRESS HEEL.

3. TRAP BALL BETWEEN GROUND AND SOLE OF FOOT.

Inside of Foot Techniques

This trap is used quite extensively. With practice a player can trap and pass with one movement.

1. KEEP EYES ON BALL.
2. BEND KNEE AND POINT TOE OUTWARD.
3. TRAP BALL BETWEEN GROUND AND INSIDE OF FOOT.
4. PROJECT UPPER BODY FORWARD.

Outside of Instep Techniques

Immediately after ball is trapped, sweep the ball around to position it for a dribble or pass.

1. KEEP EYES ON BALL.
2. SWING TRAPPING FOOT ACROSS BODY.
4. LEAN BODY AWAY FROM BALL.

3. TRAP BALL BETWEEN GROUND AND OUTSIDE OF INSTEP.
5. SWEEP BALL IN POSITION FOR PASS OR DRIBBLE.

trapping balls in mid-air

Inside of Foot Techniques

Impact point is the same as for the *inside foot* kick. Keep your eyes on the ball and body in balance. Raise the kicking foot off the ground with the inside pointing toward the descending ball. Pace is taken off the ball by recoiling the foot upon contact.

1. KEEP EYES ON BALL WITH BODY BALANCED.

2. LIFT FOOT AND POINT INSIDE OF TOE TOWARD BALL.

3. RECOIL FOOT UPON CONTACT WITH BALL.

Instep Techniques

This trap requires quick reflexes and often proves difficult.

Shift weight to non-trapping leg, bending slightly at the knee. Raise trapping leg as far as possible from the hip while bending the knee. Keep foot flexible and contact the ball with the full instep.

Drop foot rapidly at first, then slow descent as foot and ball near ground. This action takes the pace off the ball permitting the ball to land on the ground within one or two feet of the kicking foot.

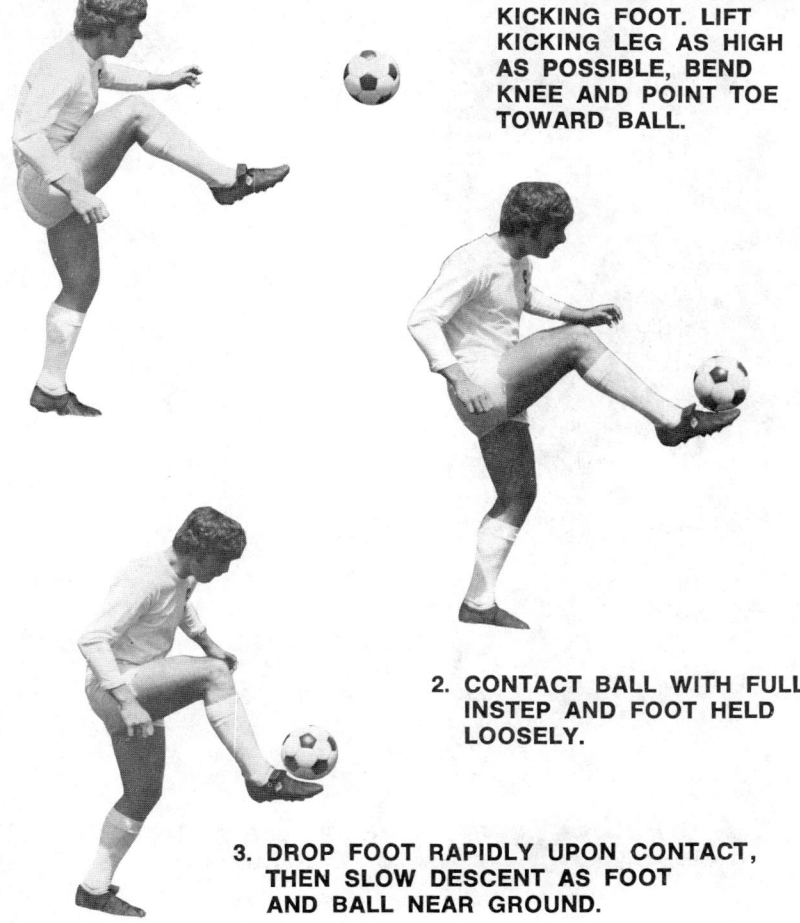

1. SHIFT WEIGHT TO NON-KICKING FOOT. LIFT KICKING LEG AS HIGH AS POSSIBLE, BEND KNEE AND POINT TOE TOWARD BALL.

2. CONTACT BALL WITH FULL INSTEP AND FOOT HELD LOOSELY.

3. DROP FOOT RAPIDLY UPON CONTACT, THEN SLOW DESCENT AS FOOT AND BALL NEAR GROUND.

Thigh Techniques

Contact the ball at the midpoint of the thigh which is raised to a horizontal level. Recoil thigh at the moment of contact.

1. KEEP EYES ON BALL.

2. LIFT LEG TO HORIZONTAL LEVEL TO CONTACT BALL AT MIDPOINT OF THIGH.

3. RECOIL LEG AT MOMENT OF CONTACT.

Chest Trap Techniques

Always be careful to keep your arms away from the ball.

With one foot kept in front of the other, arch the trunk of your body backward. Align chest with oncoming ball. Recoil upon contact and let the ball fall to the ground.

1. SPACE FEET APART WITH ONE FOOT AHEAD OF THE OTHER.

2. ARCH TRUNK BACK WHILE HUNCHING SHOULDERS FORWARD SLIGHTLY.

3. TRAP BALL IN ARCHED POSITION. RECOIL UPON CONTACT. LET BALL FALL TO GROUND.

heading

Heading Techniques

Heading is projecting the ball using the middle or side of the forehead for purposes of passing, shooting or clearing.

As the ball approaches the heading area, keep your eyes on ball, bend knees slightly and spread feet apart for balance. Move the trunk backward from the hips. Just before ball contact, tighten neck muscles and move head and trunk forward. Keep your eyes on ball throughout contact as many players make a major mistake in closing their eyes just before contact.

In heading a ball sideways, rotate the body and turn the head in the direction which the ball is to travel.

      1. KEEP EYES ON BALL THROUGHOUT CONTACT.

2. FLEX KNEES WITH LEGS APART.
3. BEND TRUNK BACKWARD FROM HIPS.
4. DRIVE TRUNK AND NECK FORWARD.
5. CONTACT BALL WITH FOREHEAD.

Backheading Techniques

Backheading is often used by forwards to pass the ball when heading conventionally becomes impractical because of an opponent's strong challenge.

Practice from a standing position at first then practice from a jump. Bend knees and move head and trunk slightly backward. Contact the ball with the upper portion of the forehead. Upon contact, straighten knees and push forward from the hips.

1. KEEP EYES ON BALL THROUGH CONTACT. FLEX KNEES WITH LEGS APART.

2. BEND HEAD AND TRUNK BACKWARD.

3. CONTACT BALL WITH UPPER PORTION OF FOREHEAD. STRAIGHTEN KNEES AND PUSH HIPS FORWARD UPON CONTACT.

dribbling

Dribbling Techniques

Dribbling is an individual skill consisting of a player's moving the ball with all portions of the foot. Although dribbling usually slows down an attack, many situations merit use of the dribble. When moving the ball by dribbling, take relatively short steps and never let the ball get further away than about one yard from the foot. If an opponent challenges from the side, move the ball to the leg farthest from the opponent.

1. USE ALL PORTIONS OF FOOT. 2. TAKE SHORT STRIDES.

3. CARRY WEIGHT ON NON-DRIBBLING FOOT. KEEP EYES ON BALL.

4. KEEP BALL WITHIN ONE YARD OF FEET.

Single Feint Techniques

Feinting while dribbling is a means of eluding an opponent. Learn to watch your opponents and teammates while still maintaining control over the ball.

Step in the direction of the feint. As the opponent reacts, reverse your direction and proceed.

1. STEP IN DIRECTION OF FEINT.

2. AS OPPONENT REACTS, REVERSE DIRECTION AND PROCEED.

Double Feint Techniques

Both single and double feints are easy to practice. For a *double feint,* step in the direction of the first feint. When the opponent does not react, feint in the opposite direction. As the opponent reacts, reverse your direction and proceed.

1. STEP IN DIRECTION OF FIRST FEINT.
2. WHEN OPPONENT DOESN'T REACT, FEINT IN OPPOSITE DIRECTION.

3. AS OPPONENT REACTS, REVERSE DIRECTION AND PROCEED.

tackling

Tackling Techniques

Tackling is a method of taking the ball away from an opponent. Tackle quickly and strongly at the moment the opponent receives the ball. If the opponent has control of the ball, "jockey" the player and watch for the moment that the ball is pushed forward. At this point, the ball is not controlled by the opponent and can be attacked or tackled.

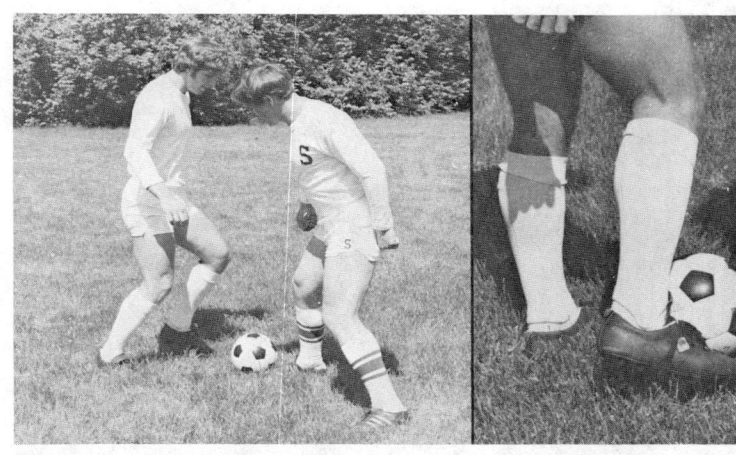

1. BLOCK BALL WITH TACKLING FOOT.
2. WEIGHT ON NON-TACKLING LEG.
3. KNEES ARE BENT.
4. PUSH BALL THROUGH WITH TACKLING FOOT.

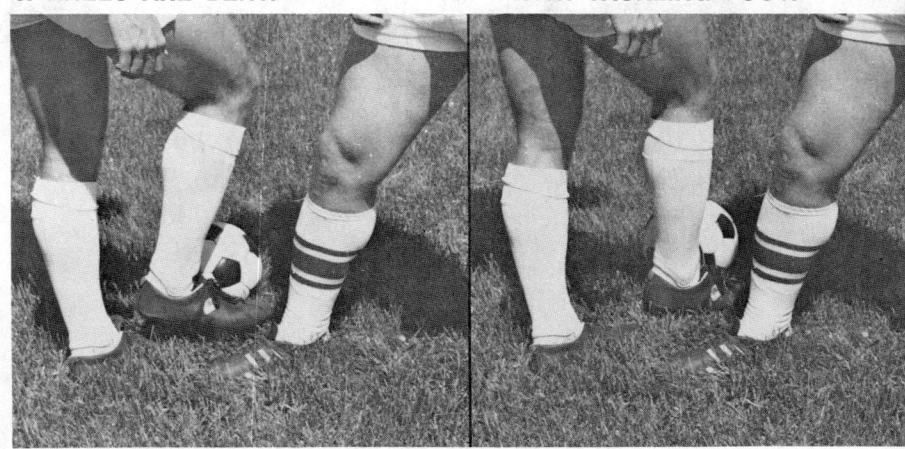

Shoulder Tackle Techniques

A *shoulder tackle* or *charge* is used to depose an opponent from the ball. The approach may be from the front or side, must be made shoulder to shoulder and cannot be violent.

Time the charge when the opponent's weight shifts to his outside foot. Hold the arm closest to opponent near to your side. Failure to do so results in a penalty for pushing.

1. APPLY BASIC TACKLING TECHNIQUES.
2. TIME TACKLE WHEN OPPONENT'S WEIGHT SHIFTS TO HIS OUTSIDE FOOT.

3. TUCK ARM NEAREST OPPONENT TO SIDE.
4. SLIDE ACROSS OPPONENT'S PATH PUSHING BALL AWAY.

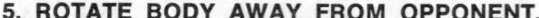
5. ROTATE BODY AWAY FROM OPPONENT.

Sliding Tackle Techniques

A *sliding tackle* is used as a last resort usually at one time or another by defenders. Be sure to contact the ball and not the opponent's feet.

Approach opponent from an oblique direction. Execute tackle only when opponent's inside leg is extended backward. Slide across and in front of your opponent to push or kick the ball out of play with the foot farthest away from the opponent.

1. APPLY BASIC TACKLING TECHNIQUES.

2. APPROACH BALL FROM OBLIQUE DIRECTION.

3. MAKE TACKLE WITH LEG FARTHEST FROM OPPONENT.

4. CONTACT BALL WHEN OPPONENT'S LEG IS BACK.

the throw-in

1. GRIP HANDS TO SIDE AND BEHIND BALL.

Throw-In Techniques

A *throw-in* must be made on or behind the touch line with both feet on the ground at the time of the throw. The ball also must be thrown from over and behind the head with both hands.

Running Throw-In Techniques

Techniques are essentially the same, except that a five to six-yard run precedes the throw. Be sure that part of the back foot stays on the ground. Learn to "drag" the back foot.

2. USE STAGGERED STANCE WITH FEET APPROXIMATELY 12 INCHES APART.

3. LEAN TRUNK BACKWARD. KNEES ARE BENT.

4. BEND ELBOWS WITH BALL BEHIND HEAD.

5. DRIVE TRUNK FORWARD AND STRAIGHTEN ARMS.

6. FOLLOW THROUGH TO TARGET.

goalkeeper catching

The goalkeeper must be able to handle balls kicked in his direction. This may be accomplished in various ways depending upon the angle from which the ball approaches. The biggest problem is learning to cut down the angle of the ball.

Catching Ground Balls Head On

When *catching ground balls head on,* face the approaching ball with feet together and legs straight. As the ball approaches, bend at the waist allowing arms to drop with palms facing ball and fingers spread. Hands are held close together and elbows are tucked toward the body. Give with hands as the ball makes contact. From this point bring the ball to your chest.

1. WITH LEGS STRAIGHT, BEND AT WAIST.

2. FEET IN LINE CLOSE TOGETHER.

3. HANDS TOGETHER, PALMS FACING BALL.

4. ELBOWS IN. KEEP EYES ON BALL.

5. DRAW BALL TO CHEST.

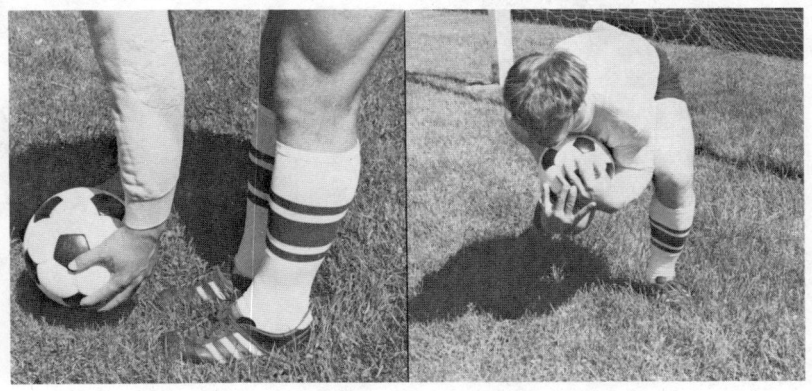

Catching Ground Balls to the Side

When *catching ground balls to the side,* take a step with the foot toward the direction of the ball and assume a kneeling position. The heel of opposite foot is positioned close to the kneeling leg. Behind the hands, the thigh and shins seal off the ball from the goal. Arm and hand positions are the same as for catching straight-on ground balls.

1. TAKE LEAD STEP TOWARD BALL.
2. DROP KNEE CLOSE TO LEAD FOOT.
3. HOLD HANDS CLOSE TOGETHER WITH PALMS FACING BALL.
4. ELBOWS IN.
5. KEEP EYES ON BALL.
6. DRAW BALL TO CHEST.

Catching Medium-High Balls

When *catching medium-high balls* waist to shoulder high, face the ball with feet seven to nine inches apart and knees slightly bent. Project arms forward with palms up and elbows bent. As ball makes contact with the arms and chest, the trunk recoils slightly to reduce the shock of the ball's contact. Pull the ball into your body for protection.

1. ARMS FORWARD, ELBOWS BENT, PALMS UP.

2. UPON CONTACT, DRAW BALL TO CHEST.

3. FORM PROTECTIVE POCKET WITH CHEST, ARMS AND HANDS.

Catching Overhead Balls

Catching overhead balls depends a great deal upon timing the approach and jump for the ball. As the ball approaches the goal, flex knees in preparation for upward extension. Drive body upward with full arm extension. Hold hands close together with palms facing ball. Catch ball with the fingers and draw the ball to a protective position.

1. FLEX KNEES.
2. EXTEND BODY UPWARD.
3. FULL ARM EXTENSION.
4. HANDS CLOSE TOGETHER, PALMS FACING BALL.
5. CATCH BALL WITH FINGERS.  
6. DRAW BALL TO PROTECTIVE POSITION.

Punching Ball and Deflecting Ball over Crossbar Techniques

If unable to catch the ball because of interference from an opposing player, you may choose to punch the ball with one or both fists rather than attempt a catch. This strategy may be especially helpful if the ball appears to be dropping under the crossbar.

Contact the ball at the height of your jump on the flat portion of your knuckle. Straighten your arms upon contact and deflect the ball toward the touch line.

1. KEEP EYES ON BALL.
2. TIME JUMP TO CONTACT BALL AT HEIGHT OF JUMP.
3. CONTACT BALL WITH ONE OR BOTH FISTS AT FLAT PORTION OF FIST.
4. DEFLECT BALL TOWARD TOUCH LINE.

Diving for High Balls and Low Balls

Even when you are positioned properly, a ball still may be out of reach making a diving catch necessary. In diving you must catch the ball or clear the ball with a punch. When making either high- or low-diving catches apply similar techniques while adjusting for the height of the ball.

Drive body with legs toward ball achieving full body extension. Forearms and palms should face the approaching ball. Catch the ball with the fingers and bring the ball to the body. "Cradle" the ball between the arms and legs. After landing roll over to protect the ball and body from the oncoming forwards.

High Ball Techniques

1. DRIVE LEGS AND ARMS UPWARD.
2. KEEP EYES ON BALL.
3. CATCH BALL WITH PALMS AND FINGERS.
4. DRAW BALL TO CHEST.

5. LAND ON SIDE.

6. ROLL TO PROTECT BALL AND BODY.

Low Ball Techniques

1. **DRIVE LEGS AND ARMS TOWARD BALL.**
2. **FULL BODY EXTENSION.**
3. **FOREARMS AND PALMS FACING BALL.** 
4. **DRAW BALL TO CHEST.** 
5. **ROLL TO PROTECT BALL AND BODY.**

45

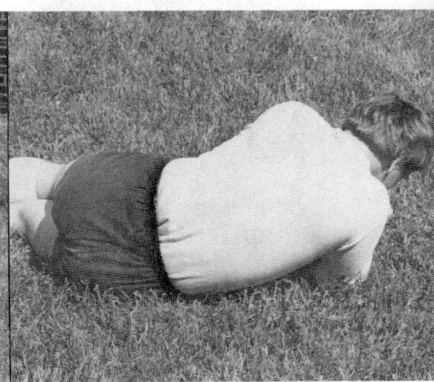

goalkeeper clearing

A goalkeeper has several methods to clear the ball out of the goal area. These include *throwing underhanded, throwing overhanded* or *punting the ball*. The method used depends on ability and the situation of the game.

Underhand Clearing Techniques

Rolling the ball along the ground is a good clearing method because it keeps the ball on the ground, permitting a teammate to gain control easily.

Always keep your eyes on the intended target. Step to the target, release the ball on the ground and follow through.

1. STEP TOWARD TARGET.

2. RELEASE BALL ON GROUND.

3. FOLLOW THROUGH TO TARGET.

Overhead Clearing Techniques

Use this clearing method for throws to long-distance targets.

Step to target, release the ball overhead and follow through to target.

1. STEP TOWARD TARGET.

2. RELEASE BALL OVERHAND.

3. FOLLOW THROUGH TO TARGET.

Punt Clearing Techniques

The method used to clear the ball for greatest distance.

Always shield the ball from oncoming opponents. Extend arms to drop the ball from about waist high. Keep your eyes on the ball. Lock the knee of the kicking leg and extend the toe. Contact the ball and follow through.

1. EXTEND ARMS. DROP BALL, DON'T THROW.
2. KEEP EYES ON BALL.
3. LOCK KNEE, EXTEND TOES.   4. FOLLOW THROUGH.

Diagram of Field

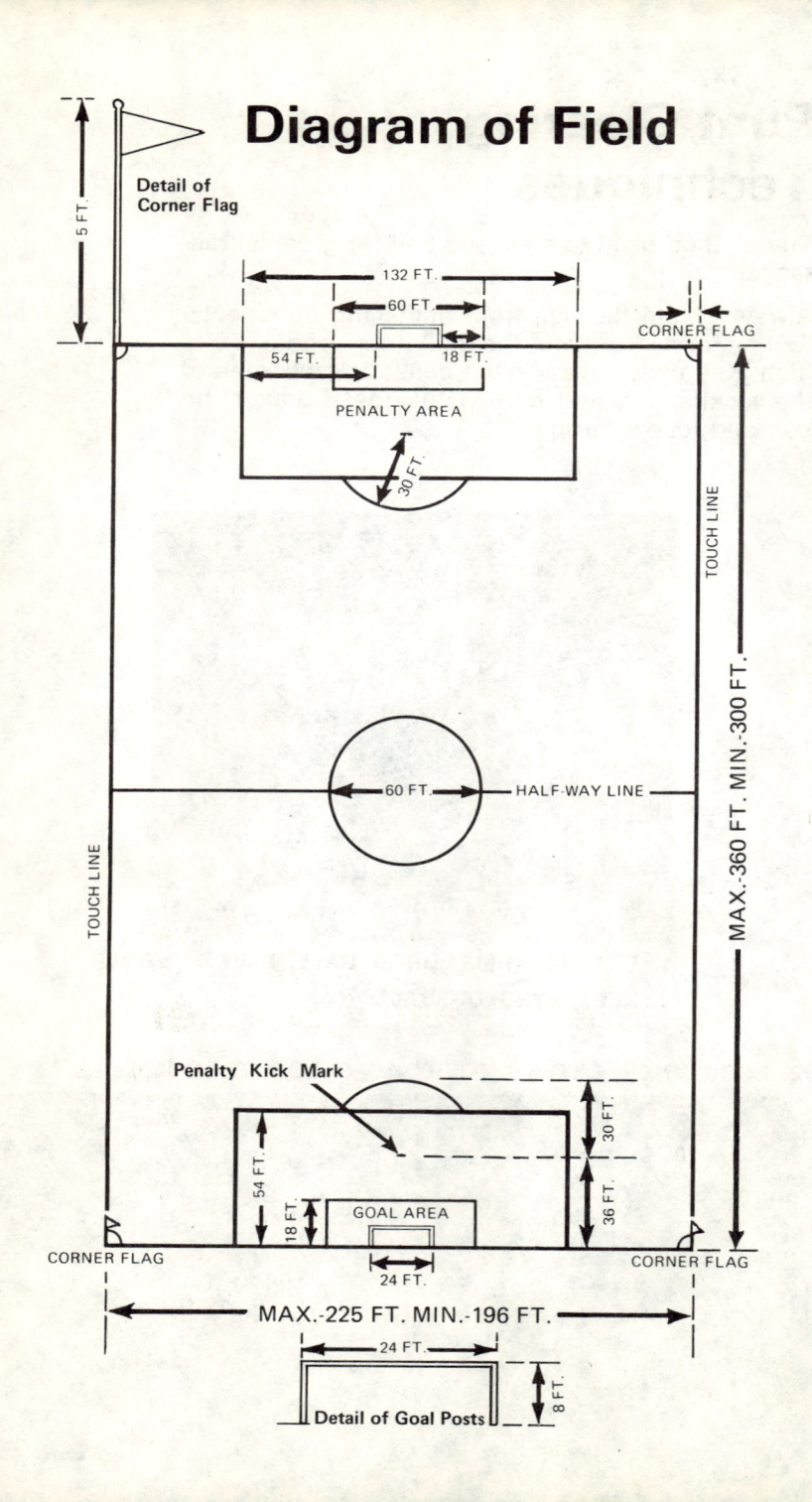

rules simplified

Sources of Soccer Rules:

SCHOOLS AND COLLEGES:
NCAA Soccer Guide
College Athletics Publishing Service
349 East Thomas Road
Phoenix, Arizona 85012

INTERNATIONAL RULES:
George Fishwick, Chairman
United States Soccer Football Assn.
350 Fifth Avenue
New York, New York 10001

WOMEN'S RULES:
DGWS Official Soccer Guide
Division for Girls' and Women's Sports
1201 Sixteenth St., N.W.
Washington, D.C. 20036

Basic Rules of Soccer

The following is a short synopsis of soccer rules. A more thorough digest can be obtained by referring to the above-mentioned publications.

Line-up

Eleven men are on a side. The offense consists of five men: one *center*, two *insides*, and two *wingers*. Two *halfbacks* operate at mid-field between the forwards and the defense. Halfbacks both attack and defend depending upon the situation. Three *fullbacks* and a *goalkeeper* make up the defensive unit. The goalkeeper is the only man who can use his hands and may do so only in the penalty area.

Field Dimensions

The recommended size of a soccer field for adults is between 70 and 80 yards wide and 110 to 120 yards in length. It is somewhat less for younger ages. The goal is 8 x 24 feet.

Time

In association soccer there are two 45-minute halves. Collegiate rules provide for four 22-minute quarters. There are no team time-outs in soccer; however, the referee may call time for an injury. Substitutions are made quickly on throw-ins, goal kicks and corner kicks.

Scoring

A goal is scored when the whole ball passes over the goal line between the uprights and under the crossbar. Any part of the body except the hands and arms can be used to propel the ball into the goal. Each goal counts one point regardless of how it is achieved.

Fouls

An indirect free kick is awarded for non-personal fouls such as dangerous play, a goalkeeper taking too many steps with the ball and offsides.

A second player from either team must touch the ball on an indirect kick before a goal can be scored. A goal cannot be scored directly from the kicker's foot.

Direct Free Kicks

These kicks are awarded providing a personal foul is committed such as pushing, holding, kicking, kneeing, elbowing an opponent or intentionally handling the ball. A goal can be scored directly from a kick awarded for foregoing reasons. If the foul occurs within the penalty area, a penalty kick is awarded. Penalty kicks are taken from a spot 12 yards in front of goal.

Offside

The offside rule prevents players from being "basket hangers" or "sleepers" as in basketball. A player in his opponent's end of the field must have two opponents between himself and the goal line at the time the ball is played to him.

Goal Kicks

Such are awarded to the defending team if the attacking team kicks or heads the ball past the end line.

Corner Kick

This kick is awarded to the attacking team when defender last touches the ball before going over the end line.

Throw-ins

When the ball goes over the touch or side line, a throw-in is awarded to the opposing team of the player who last touched the ball.

basic tactics

In any team sport, and especially in soccer, teamwork is a must. If 11 men go on the field and play as individuals, these 11 individuals will probably lose the match.

Certain attributes and skills are considered important when picking a position to play.

Goalkeeper

The goalkeeper should have good hands and be able to handle the ball cleanly. Better that a goalkeeper be fairly "rangy" which helps when diving and defending against a high cross pass, especially if the goal area is crowded.

Judgment and timing of when to come out of the goal or when to stay are essential. Goalkeepers must learn to narrow the angle of the ball to the goal, giving a forward the least space in which to shoot. For example, if a center forward had a breakaway straight down the field and the goalie stayed on the goal line so as not to move toward him, the forward would have the best possible angle from which to shoot. However, if the goalkeeper moved toward the incoming forward, the angle would be narrowed and there would be less goal space at which to shoot. The goalkeeper should keep his body behind the ball. A goalie can never relax and must be alert at all times. He never uses his feet when he can use his hands.

If possible after a shot has been stopped, it is better to throw or kick the ball to an open teammate than to kick the ball indiscriminately up field.

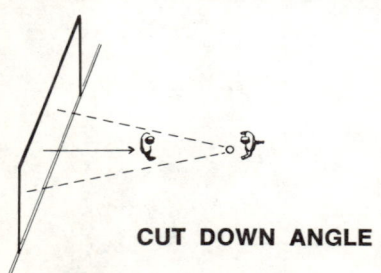

CUT DOWN ANGLE

Fullbacks

In this position the player should have the speed to stay with his winger and be a good tackler and header. Fullbacks and other defenders should understand the difference between *man to man defense* and *zone defense*. Strictly man to man defense means for instance that the fullback covers the winger and follows him no matter where he goes. In a zone defense the fullback covers a given area and keeps an eye on any player in his zone. Most teams generally use a combination of zone and man to man. The *diagonal coverage*, sometimes called *balancing the defense*, incorporates both these principles.

When the ball is on the right wing, the left back meets the attack and plays a man to man with the opposing winger while the center half and the right back cover the opponent toward the center of the field. These two men are playing a zone defense in this situation. When the ball is on the left wing, the right back meets the play and the center half and left back cover.

On corner kicks the fullbacks stand on the goal line near each goal post. Any player should look to pass to a teammate before kicking the ball up field. Often a winger or halfback is free near the touch line. However when in doubt especially within the penalty area, it's a good idea to kick the ball out. The fullbacks in most systems cover the opposing wingers to keep them from cutting to the inside.

When a player passes back to his own goalkeeper, the player should kick the ball outside either post, in the event that player makes a bad pass or the goalie misjudges the ball.

When the goalkeeper moves out for a ball, the fullback should cover the goal. On the attack fullbacks position themselves around the mid-field area.

Center Halfback

Sometimes called the *center fullback*, because his role is to block the middle of the field. He is the king pin in the defense and is probably the best defensive ball player on the team. He should possess the same skills and understanding of the game as do the fullbacks. Usually in a defensive situation he covers the opposing center forward. A tall, rangy center half who can head well is an asset to any team.

Wing Halfbacks

The wing halfback is one of the hardest working players on the field. He must be able to defend and attack. He is a link between the forwards and the defense. His job is to cover the opposing inside forward and also feed his forward line on the attack. The wing halfback along with the inside men must have tremendous stamina, ball control and strong tackling ability. His passes may be short to his other halfback and inside or long to his wingers and center forward. Frequently, he will change positions on the field, mainly with the forwards but sometimes with his fullbacks depending on the system used. A complete understanding of the game situation with his teammates is all-important if this switch is to work effectively. He should practice hard on throw-ins in game situations and be able to hit his wingers and inside men with precision.

Wing Forwards

The wing forwards are players who have great speed and ball-handling ability. They play mainly in an area 10 yds. from the touch line and should be able to use both feet, either for crosses or for shots at the goal. A wing forward must defend when his defense is under pressure and move to the attack upon receiving the ball. He must work closely with his inside man and wing half. At different times during the game, he will switch with other forwards. Some wingers make the mistake of thinking that they are on the field only to attack. So they stand on the mid-field line while their defense is being pressed.

Inside Forwards

Along with the wing halfbacks, the inside forwards have one of the most grueling positions on the field. They attempt to open the way for the center forward and the two wingers, and generally play a trailing position to these three players. A center forward defends as well as attacks and covers the opposing wing halfs. He must go through on his own at times and be able to shoot when given the opening. During a game, he may switch with the center forward or winger forward. This gives the inside man welcome rest from his strenuous midfield duties; however, this can be done only when each position understands the other players' roles.

Center Forward

The center forward is the spearhead of the attack and usually has the best position on the field to score goals. He must bring his insides and wingers into the play with well-timed passes and be able to shoot with either foot. Because he is very closely marked by the opposing center fullback, he can "decoy" himself to pull the defender out, thus allowing his inside man to go through. He changes positions frequently with the winger and must think about playing the ball across the field as well as down the field. He should be a good header since many scoring opportunities will arise from crosses from the wing. Many center forwards spend too much time in the middle of the field. They should change positions with other forwards and always look for scoring opportunities.

systems of play

One of the most basic offensive and defensive patterns for beginners is the *MW formation.*

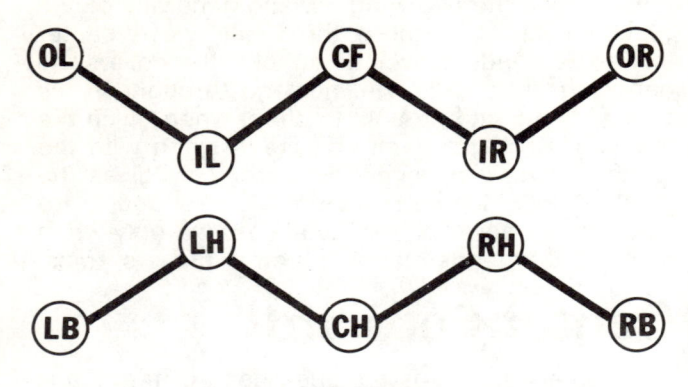

MW FORMATION

The three fullbacks and the wing halfbacks form the M of the formation. The W is formed by the insides, wingers, and center forward. This formation covers the field well and gives depth to the offense and defense.

In this formation the defensive coverage is comprised of fullbacks on the wingers, wing halfbacks covering the opposing inside man, and the center half or center fullback covering the center forward. Variations of this offensive pattern constitute the *Inverted W formation* which retains the three-back defense.

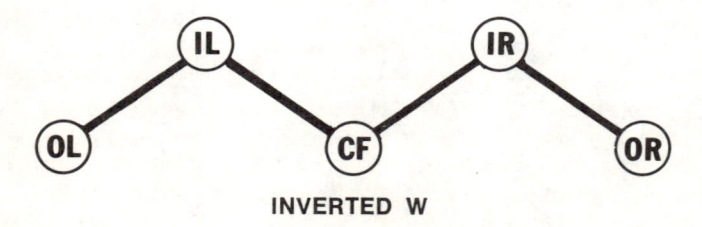

INVERTED W

In this formation, the center forward assumes a position in line with the wingers. If the defense challenges with fullbacks on the wingers, halfbacks on the inside men and the center half covering the center forward, the opposition is then in a defense which it is not accustomed to playing. It means the center half moves more into the midfield and cannot play his "stopper" position. The fullbacks are pulled out of their normal position and moved farther up field to challenge the wingers. The halfbacks are now playing a "stopper role" because the opposing inside men are playing a double center forward position. All of this creates problems for the opposing defense. Intelligent forwards sometimes can capitalize on this situation before the other team can adjust.

Another formation called the *4-2-4 system* is very popular with experienced teams throughout the world.

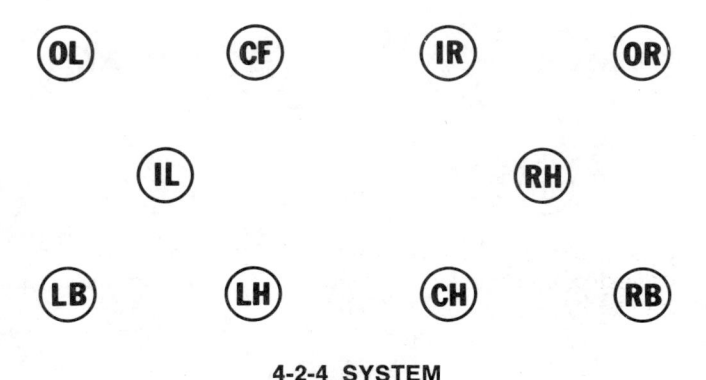

(OL)   (CF)   (IR)   (OR)

    (IL)   (RH)

(LB)   (LH)   (CH)   (RB)

4-2-4 SYSTEM

To play this formation a team must have two link men who can attack with the four forwards and then defend with the four backs. This formation gives a team six forwards on offense and six men on defense. The link position requires tremendous stamina and skill. For this reason, beginning soccer teams may find this formation difficult. The success of a team using this system rests almost totally on these two middle men.

There are variations of the 4-2-4, namely the *defensive 4-3-3* and the *offensive 3-3-4*. These two systems are accomplished from the 4-2-4 by moving one man to mid-field from the four backs or the four forwards, depending upon whether the team needs defensive or offensive strength.

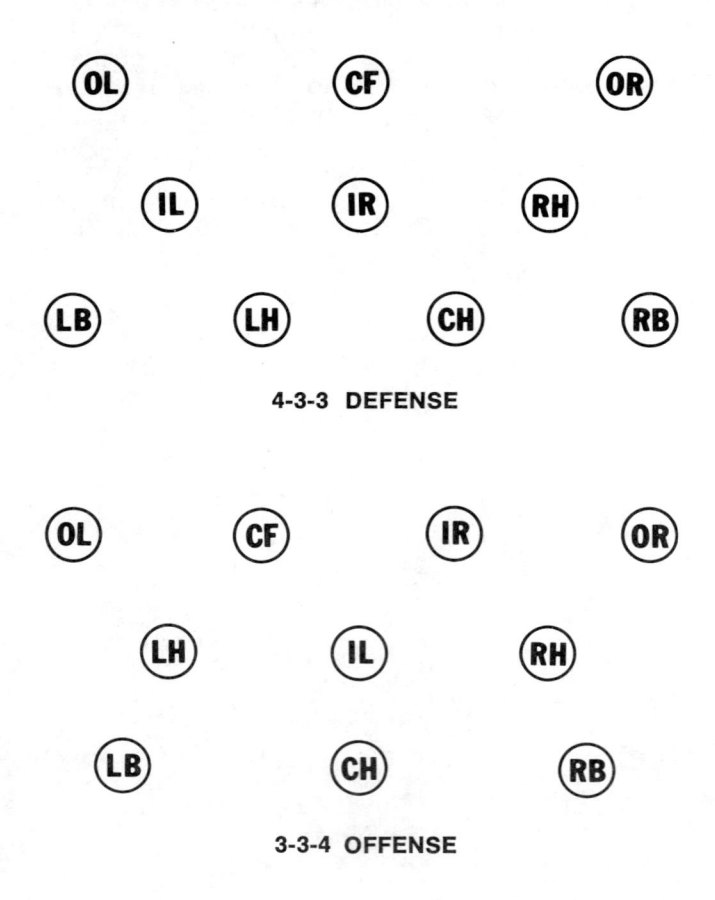

(OL)   (CF)   (OR)

        (IL)   (IR)   (RH)

(LB)   (LH)   (CH)   (RB)

4-3-3 DEFENSE

(OL)   (CF)   (IR)   (OR)

        (LH)   (IL)   (RH)

(LB)   (CH)   (RB)

3-3-4 OFFENSE

In selecting a system, the formation must be compatible with the players. A coach should never attempt to force a particular formation upon his players. Also, a formation is not rigidly held throughout the game. It is only a framework through which different plays are worked. After each play has terminated, the players move back into formation.

Soccer is played with the men positioned in a series of interlocking triangles which add depth to both the offense and defense. This means that forwards and defense men must not attack or defend on a "flat front." In a situation where three backs stand in a straight line across the field, none of the three can cover the space behind each of the other players on a through pass. Furthermore, four forwards attacking in a straight line across the field limit the passing possibilities.

As in any team game the more that the players practice together, the better the system works. Each man must completely understand his role in the formation. Also, he must have a knowledge of the duties of the men around him. Only then can he be expected to function effectively as a member of the team.

External Factors Which Affect the Game

Size of Field

A narrow field tends to favor the defense because there is less space for the attacker to work and consequently less space for defenders to cover. Large fields help well-conditioned teams. On small fields conditioning plays a lesser role because of restricted space.

Playing Surface

On grassy fields the ball bounces "more true" and it's easier to control. However, a long ball may skid. On a hard field the ball bounces high and is much more difficult to control. If the field is covered with ice and snow it is naturally quite slippery. Players must run with a low center of gravity to change directions easily. Muddy or snow-covered fields generally are favorable to strong players. Under these conditions, the ball cannot be passed along the ground. As a result, long passes and lob passes must be used.

Wind

If the day happens to be windy, a player passing the ball into the wind must keep the ball low. If the wind is strong toward the corner kick, the kicker should make a 10 or 15 yd. pass to a halfback or inside man rather than a long center.

Sun

The direction from which the sun is shining is a factor to consider when choosing goals to defend at the start of the game. One team will have to defend with the sun in its eyes. If the ball is wet, the goalkeeper should wear gloves to aid in gripping the ball. When the sun shines into the goalkeeper's eyes, a visored cap should be worn.

Helpful Hints for Players

1. Don't dribble when you can make a constructive pass.

2. Move to the open spot—move away from your defender—so you are in a better position to receive the ball.

3. When a defender is pressed, kick the ball downfield or over the touch line.

4. When the ball is lost from view, all forwards should think defensively.

5. Make constructive passes across the field and behind as well as in front.

6. Defenders can back pass to the goalkeeper as a safety maneuver. Pass to the outside of the goal mouth.

7. Make the easy play. Allow the ball to work for you. Don't you work for the ball.

8. Wing forwards should stay wide and close to the touch line. This brings the defender out in the middle of the field and allows more open space for your attack.

9. Don't be afraid to talk to your teammates on the field. Let them know what is happening in the area around them which their field of vision cannot pick up.

10. As a defender faced with two or more opponents, retreat slowly, giving more time for teammates to come back to help.

11. Forwards should switch positions at various times during the game with other members of the forward line—example, center forward with winger. This sometimes confuses the defense.

12. Never retreat with your back to the ball. Watch the ball at all times.

13. As a defender, stay between ball and goal.

14. The closer the play develops toward your own goal, the tighter the defense.

15. As a defender challenge only when you have a good chance to obtain the ball.

16. Defenders should have restraint and control. Let your opponent commit himself first.

17. Delaying principles are good tactics in defense. This means slowing down the opponent's forward line.

18. Back up teammates and help cover the space behind fellow players.

19. Always move toward the pass, don't wait for the pass to come to you.

20. A most important thing to learn is quickness off the mark. The first three or four steps are all-important in soccer. Beat your opponent to the ball.

21. What you do without the ball is as important as what you do with the ball.

22. A well-placed shot is more effective than a hard shot.

23. An effective player is always in good physical shape.

24. Play the ball, not the man.

25. Respect the referee's decision.

glossary of soccer terms

CLEARING: The act of moving the ball from within scoring range. A defensive measure.

CORNER KICK. A *direct free kick* taken by the offensive team from the one-yard arc at the corner of field.

COVER: To take a position close to your opponent so as to challenge his efforts.

DIRECT FREE KICK: A place kick which can score directly from the kicker's foot.

DRIBBLING: A way of moving the ball along the ground by using the feet while keeping the ball under player's control.

FEINTING: A body movement or swaying away from intended direction. A deliberately deceptive movement.

FLAT FRONT: Players attacking or defending in straight line across field.

GOAL: When the ball passes completely over goal line and under cross bar, one point is scored per goal.

GOAL KICK: An *indirect kick* taken by the defensive team from the half of the goal area closest to where the ball crossed over the end line.

HALF VOLLEY: To kick the ball the instant after it touches the ground. Kicking the ball on the short hop.

HEADING: An act of directing the ball with any part of your forehead.

INDIRECT FREE KICK: A place kick which will not score a goal unless touched or played by one other player before going into the goal.

JOCKEY: A way of covering the man with the ball by feinting without committing yourself.

OFFSIDES: A player being nearer to his opponent's goal line than the ball at the moment the ball is played. For exceptions consult rule book.

PENALTY AREA: At each end of the soccer field two lines are drawn at right angles to the goal line, 18 yards from each goal post. Lines also extend into the field of play for a distance of 15 yards and are joined by a line drawn parallel with the goal post.

RECOIL: To draw back part of body upon contact with ball. This absorbs the shock on impact.

TACKLING: Taking the ball from your opponent by using the feet.

TRAPPING: The act of stopping a ball and bringing the ball under your control.

TOUCH LINE: The side lines of the field.

notes

notes